MW01294127

RIGHT SIDE UP

Is a Better Life Possible?

CRAIG L. MORRIS

WESTBOW
PRESS®
A DIVISION OF THOMAS NELSON
& ZONDERVAN

Scripture taken from the Holy Bible, NEW INTERNATIONAL VERSION®. Copyright © 1973, 1978, 1984 by Biblica, Inc. All rights reserved worldwide. Used by permission. NEW INTERNATIONAL VERSION® and NIV® are registered trademarks of Biblica, Inc. Use of either trademark for the offering of goods or services requires the prior written consent of Biblica US, Inc.

This book is a work of non-fiction. Unless otherwise noted, the author and the publisher make no explicit guarantees as to the accuracy of the information contained in this book and in some cases, names of people and places have been altered to protect their privacy.

Interior Graphics/Art Credit: Sophia Louise Morris and Stephanie Norman.

WestBow Press books may be ordered through booksellers or by contacting:

WestBow Press
A Division of Thomas Nelson & Zondervan
1663 Liberty Drive
Bloomington, IN 47403
www.westbowpress.com
1 (866) 928-1240

Cover design credit: Rodjie P. Ulanday
And shutterstock

ISBN: 978-1-5127-4009-7 (sc)
ISBN: 978-1-5127-4010-3 (hc)
ISBN: 978-1-5127-4008-0 (e)

Library of Congress Control Number: 2016906792

Print information available on the last page.

WestBow Press rev. date: 07/07/2016

Contents

Dedication

I dedicate this book to my loving family...

Hal & Connie, two of the most loving and supportive parents for which a son could ask.

Deb, my sweet sister who has a heart of pure gold.

Cherish, my precious wife who has the strength and tenderness necessary to pull greatness out of me and others.

Sophia and Alexa, God's tremendous blessings in the form of two amazing daughters! You both bring light, joy and inspiration wherever you go! I pray that your love for God and others would continue to grow all of your days!

Introduction

My eyes were riveted on the three plane formation racing across the blue sky. Suddenly, the plane on the right pealed off and soared up into the sky until it was no longer visible. A tear ran down my cheek. I stood mere feet from the coffin wrapped body of my dear friend who had just ended his 3-month battle with cancer. As a businessman, pilot and flight instructor, flying was one of his passions. The decision was made to honor the life he lived by having three of his former students fly what is called the "missing man formation." Watching that lonely plane sail into the blue sky created one of those rare, soul impacting moments that compels us to ask important questions:

> Am I making the most of my life?
> Am heading in the right direction?
> What are people going to say about me after I'm gone?
> Are my relationships in a good place?
> If that were me, where would I be right now?

These questions all seem to point to one key, life-changing question, "Am I living life Right Side Up?"

> *"Life is a daring adventure or nothing at all."*
> Helen Keller

What is the "Right Side Up" life?

Surrounded by people who seem to be living life upside down, sometimes it's easier to observe someone living Right Side Up than it is to describe with words. Even if it's only in hints, whispers and shadows of what could be, we are fairly certain when we see life being lived Right Side Up. Many words and phrases can be used for it: healthy, blessed, connected, a life by design or living abundantly. It is the prevailing force in our heart that beckons us towards better lives and relationships. There is a yearning in our hearts that longs for joy, peace, a life lived well–Right Side Up.

The true challenge isn't identifying what a great life looks like–it's moving towards one. And though we may differ on some smaller out-workings, there seems to be a consensus agreement on what the right rhythm of life looks like and feels like. Most of us want to live life Right Side Up. How do we get and keep our lives moving in the right direction with the right trajectory?

Q: If you had to be someone else, someone you know well, who would you choose to be?

Chances are, this person embodies qualities of the life you desire. I've asked this question to hundreds of people over the years. Answers have ranged from the meaningful to the hilarious. People with intellectual virtue will identify a person they admire and share stories of how they have been impacted and inspired by this person. People wanting to sidestep a tough question might quickly quip, "I'd like to be my spouse so I could be married to me!" As the laughter and the Cheshire cat smile drifts away the question calling us towards a great life still remains.

My friend who died of cancer, lived life Right Side Up. Simply put, he gave the right percent of his heart and soul to the right things. He wasn't perfect, but he worked hard, loved deeply, pursued personal health and healing and learned how to connect well with both God and those who were near to him. We met weekly for over two years. It was during that time that we raised questions, had conversations at a soul level and helped each other move towards the best life possible. Like me, he had a hopeful and inquisitive heart. Individually and collectively we experienced part of the journey towards the Right Side Up life.

THE PATH

Q: How do you begin moving towards a Right Side Up life?

I'd love to promise you that this book will totally transform your life. It can't. Only you have the ability to make the changes necessary to go through a challenging and beautiful metamorphosis. What this book can do for you is provide you with the opportunity to work hard, live a great life and see your life continually improve over time.

Q: Would you be happy if your life and relationships got 2% better each month?

Think of that! Over time, this is revolutionary life-change. Below are four of the things you need for your journey towards Right Side Up!

#1 You need GREAT QUESTIONS.

Q: Is a better life possible?

Now that's a great question! Sit with that question for a few minutes and let it take you to a place of wonder, curiosity, inspiration and potentially even action. Can you believe it? All of that activity fueled by a simple question–your heart, mind, soul, and spirit did the rest.

> *"The first key to wisdom is constant and frequent questioning, for by doubting we are led to question and by questioning we arrive at the truth."*
> Peter Abelard

What if I told you that it is actually the questions, not the answers, which could be the key to unlocking the full, satisfying, abundant life you truly seek—for which your heart longs? The truth is that every single day, you ask and respond to hundreds of questions ranging from the mundane or annoying to the essential and meaningful. If you have ever parented or spent even an hour with a two-year-old, you know that it is our very nature to ask questions. But there are good questions and there are great questions. The quality of the questions you ask will determine the quality of your life.

Good questions are thought provoking. Like receiving a new toy on a childhood birthday, a good question captures your attention, gets your juices flowing and helps you to think of important life matters in a new light, from a different angle. Unfortunately, like a new toy, the newness of a good question will often wear off and lack the ability to prod you into a new actionable direction.

> *"The ability to ask the right question is more than half*
> *the battle of finding the answer."*
> John Maxwell

Great questions move us towards our life goals and dreams. They help us to live the life we've always wanted, inspiring us to concurrently live an extraordinary life as an individual while simultaneously allowing us to experience fantastic relationships with those around us. If we want to live the best life possible, we need to learn how to consistently and regularly ask wise, helpful and great questions!

In the Bible, there is a story of two religious leaders walking past a badly beaten and injured man. A third man, a foreigner, asked a great question and was moved towards compassionate action which undoubtedly changed his life and the life of the abandoned man. Consider these comments from Martin Luther King Jr. about the story of the good Samaritan: *The first question the priest and the Levite asked was: "If I stop to help this man, what will happen to ME?" But...the good Samaritan reversed the question: "If I do not stop to help this man, what will happen to HIM?"*

Q: What if life changing power rested in the asking of great questions?

- A high output individual, perpetually sprinting on the treadmill of life, seeks out a thoughtful counselor in order to find, "The next level." They hear an unexpected and life altering question: *"Maybe the 'Next level,' is learning how to enjoy this level first?"*
- An estranged parent and child are at an impasse between two bad options. A wise coach shares a questions that opens up a ray of hope, *"Maybe there is a third way?"*
- A severely abused woman is distraught, depressed and despondent at her current circumstances. An empathetic, encouraging and knowledgeable friend asks, *"Have you ever overcome something like this before?"*
- Two divorced parents are ruining their daughter's wedding rehearsal because of their fears, wounds and selfishness. An insightful pastor pulls them aside and inquires, *"Do you want this wedding day to be the best day possible for the daughter you love?"*
- A separated man receives a scathing letter from his estranged wife. The note lists all of the hurtful things he has done *to* her and not done *for* her. A sage inquires, *"Is it possible that her vulnerable sharing needs*

to be celebrated as a step towards your new level of honesty and intimacy?"

What do these all have in common? These great and meaningful questions allow us to explore life at a different and higher level. Inherent wisdom is built into a great question, enough so that a person is compelled in the direction of a life of health and vitality.

I love hearing the phrase, "That's a great question!" That statement signifies that an inquiry took someone to a place of exploration which in time, hopefully, will allow them to lean into health, healing and wholeness in relationships. The right question at the right moment can change your life!

Q: Why does the Right Side Up life require questions and not answers?

Face it: people want answers, not questions. You don't attend a class, read a book, call a friend, or risk joining a support group because you're looking for questions—clearly, it is the answers, the solutions, and the new insight that you seek. We learn from a tender age that the right answer gets the teacher's approving nod and that a collection of the most accurate answers earns the best score. Tests with right answers get posted on the refrigerators, employees with swift and creative responses get promoted, and a boyfriend who successfully responds to the question, "Do these pants make me look fat?" may be instantly elevated to relationship super-stardom.

Great questions pay off for as much as you've invested into them. Like life, simple and easy answers follow the path of least resistance, without much staying power or transforming ability. The great answers to life's great questions need to be discovered through reflection, thoughtful inquiry and participation in meaningful relationship. Here's the way curiosity and critical thinking pay off: The more questions you ask, the better solutions and options you have. The better options you have, the better life you will live. If I tell you the, "right answers," you may politely nod your head in agreement and forget our discussion five minutes later. But, if I ask you a great question, and you put in the work necessary to wrestle with the topic at hand, you will hold on tenaciously to that self-discovered nugget with a greater desire to implement your new discovery into your life.

> "You can tell whether a man is clever by his answers.
> You can tell whether a man is wise by his questions."
> Naguib Mahfouz

Q: Do you have the right questions to live the Right Side Up life?

#2 You need SPACE for growth and health.

> "To live is the rarest thing in the world.
> Most people exist, that is all."
> Oscar Wilde

It's impossible to discover the Right Side Up life when we are surrounded by noise. You don't need to be told that in our frantic, frenetic world, few of us slow down long enough to be mindful, present and reflective. But perhaps you did not know that the hurried life is a tremendous threat to the good life–the life that God has called you towards. I'm convinced that most of us are living life in the matrix, too busy, too deluded to pause long enough to create space to allow these questions to form, take root and powerfully change our lives. With the hurried pace of so many, time to reflect, be intentional and grow has all but vanished. You won't be able to solve life's problems, big or small, nor achieve your goals without margin.

Q: When is the last time you were able to sit down, grab your favorite drink, stare out a window and think?

The crowded life keeps us from asking questions. "Too busy," is the battle cry of the weary soul. Those who live a marginless life are confined to putting all of their energy into survival, never able to peek over the edge of the struggle towards thriving. We need even just a little bit of space to begin the journey towards life and health.

"Perhaps it would be a good idea, fantastic as it sounds,
to muffle every telephone, stop every motor and halt all
activity for an hour some day to give people a chance

to ponder for a few minutes on what it is all about,
why they are living and what they really want."
James Truslow Adams (1949)

The busy, upside down life compels us to ask the wrong questions. Not only are we in too much of a hurry to ask great questions, many of the questions we ask are in fact, misguided questions and will serve only to lead us down a dark rabbit hole of distraction. For many individuals, the central, subconscious questions that guide them through their day are completely self-focused and may sound like:

"How can I be most happy?"
"What will keep me safe and help me to avoid pain?"
"How can I create distance from what scares me?"
"How can I help those around me to be happy?"
"What's in it for me?"

These questions may seem nice or innocent, but such questions are built on a faulty premise—that the goal of life is to be happy, or that God's objective for each of His children is for them to *just* be happy, failing to acknowledge that we live in a broken and sinful world, deeply in need of restoration. In fact, there are fatal flaws of misaligned purposes or mistaken perspectives built into every wrong question we ask. Consider two different friends, one which is operating with the above questions and the other which is asking different, great questions like the ones contained in this book. Which friend would you rather be with? Which friend will help you live a great, Right Side Up life? One friend will be stuck in the selfish mire of "me," while the other will be able to connect and love you for who you are.

> *"It's not that they can't see the solution.*
> *They can't see the problem."*
> G.K. Chesterton

Great questions are one of the best ways possible to create space in our lives to move towards what matters most and closer to the lives we've always wanted! I used to have a question on the back of my car, "Can you love someone if you are trying to change them?" I so enjoyed inflicting this beautiful and challenging question on hundreds of preoccupied and overloaded people on the road each day! Great questions take us to a magical place of discovery, the arena where we can be guided towards a Right Side Up life!

Q: Do you have enough margin in your life to sit with the powerful questions that will change your life?

#3 We need PEOPLE to explore with.

> *"What does love look like? It has the hands to help others.*
> *It has the feet to hasten to the poor and needy. It has eyes*
> *to see misery and want. It has the ears to hear the sighs*
> *and sorrows of men. That is what love looks like."*
> St. Augustine

The pursuit of a great life, like most endeavors on which we embark, won't merely be a self-discovery exercise. I'm the first to admit, there are many times when I wish life, growth and health could be found in solitude, quiet reflection and a warm cup of coffee. Life isn't designed that way. For some reason, a good question becomes a great question when it's wrapped with skin, care and compassion. The words that come from a trusted friend or spouse will find places in my heart, mind and soul that my "self-talk," won't ever reach.

Years ago I went to a counselor and said, "Hey, this isn't going to be some long term gig for you. Tell me the books I need to read to get better, and I'll be on my way." I'm sure the counselor chuckled, thinking to herself as I now have come to understand, "Buddy, that's part of your problem!" Solitude may be good and healthy–isolation is devastating. Insulating ourselves from others when it comes to growth and healing dwarfs our maturity and keeps us from living a great life–life Right Side Up!

People are different. There are some who process internally–with a journal, on a park bench, by themselves. There are those who process externally–with a friend or loved one, in an open and safe conversation. Both of these avenues are needed to pursue a great life.

Internal and external processors need each other. Some would love personal transformation to be an independent studies course, a solo mission of getting healthier and wiser, while others would love growth to be a group project–surrounded by people, input, collaborating together towards a finished project.

The Right Side Up life, includes both *solitude*, moments of quiet reflection to discover things for yourself, and *people* to help process and reality test your experiences, observations, and conclusions.

> *"Loneliness expresses the pain of being alone and*
> *solitude expresses the glory of being alone."*
> Paul Tillich

One of my greatest, life changing experiences was meeting every week with two other like minded men. Our histories were different, but we had similar hearts, we shared like vulnerabilities and common weak spots. I hope that you can taste what I did in that season of my life: Acceptance, healing, freedom, the ability to be strong and weak, to be courageous and human, and still to be loved. I received a great gift from those men that I am now able to pass on to people I meet with on a regular basis. I so enjoy hearing this comment from those I coach and counsel, "Craig, I don't need to filter my words with you, I can just say what I think and feel and I know you'll accept me where I am." Living a Right Side Up life requires safe, healing relationships to help us on our journey.

> *"When my business partner and friend was murdered I*
> *wrestled with many questions with God. I found it is good to*
> *wrestle with God and even better when friends are involved."*
> Mike Baker

Q: Who are the companions on my journey towards the Right Side Up life?

#4 You need MOTIVATION.

The upside down life can be a powerful motivator. Regardless if it was personally experienced or learned from watching someone else destroy his life and the lives of those around him, seeing brokenness, selfishness and strife eating up a soul is a sad thing indeed. The upside down life can nudge us in a healthier direction, but it's not the best motivator. Avoidance has never been a great strategy for living a life Right Side Up. Humans are hardwired to want to move towards something, not away from something.

When it comes to movement towards goals, health and a great life, there are two motivation oriented sub-questions that you alone can answer: *Is it worth it? Can I do it?* Your current life trajectory has been pre-programmed by your beliefs about life, work, and the payoff at the end of the rainbow. The good news is that this can change!

Too many people motivate themselves out of hurt, disgust or self-hatred. They despise themselves enough to make some small changes, and over time, if they don't continue to loath themselves as much as before, they will stop the transformation process. Lasting, powerful motivation needs to flow from love and hope. People need to know they are loved, love themselves and need encouragement, hope that the changes they are implementing will bring about the life they desire.

I love to see the twinkle of light that appears in the eyes of someone when hope resurfaces. My wife and I have coached and counseled hundreds of individuals and couples over the years. Something special happens the moment they realize that their current life experience doesn't have to continue in the same rut. Their countenance changes when they begin to see a picture of a brighter future, one that is a little more free, beautiful and healthy.

Q: Do you *wish* to live a better life or *want* to live a better life?

> *"Opportunity is missed by most people because it*
> *is dressed in overalls and looks like work."*
> Thomas Edison

The Journey

Revisiting the story of my friend's memorial. People from all facets of his life gathered to share stories of how this Right Side Up life had intersected with their own. An emotional tension was created in my heart and soul. Though it was a beautiful celebration of a life, it sapped almost every ounce of my emotional energy. Wearily, I returned home that night to my energetic kids. They could tell that I wasn't my normal happy and playful self.

One of my daughters asked, "What's wrong daddy? Is everything ok?"

"Sweetheart, today I had to say my last goodbye to a good friend." I decided this would be a good time to tell them about what had happened. With a heavy heart I shared, "My good friend Dale died. We had his funeral services today. Dale is now in Heaven with Jesus."

After a long pause, my sweet little 4-year-old Alexa asked, "Daddy, is Heaven going to be like a big party?"

"Yes it is, Sweetie." Tears began to well up in my eyes. I tried to rally some excitement and with a forced smile I continued, "Yes, it's going to be a huge party! There will probably be more balloons up there than you can possibly imagine."

Alexa paused, looked up into the sky and said, "That's right! Lots of people have lost their balloons up there!"

In the same way my tiny messenger, my daughter Alexa, used our relationship and the space created to ask me a great question, my hope is that you would begin to regularly ask yourself and those around you the great questions that can heal, transform, and lead you and those around you towards the Right Side Up life! My dream for this book is that it will serve as an inspiration and encouragement for you to live a great life! This book contains some of the best questions with which God has blessed me. These questions will encourage you to explore and inspire you to live the best *life* possible, with the best *relationships* possible while connecting in the best possible way to the *God* who loves you more than you will ever know!

Are you courageous enough to embark on a journey of life and relationship transformation through the world of questions?

Are you ready to make the world around you better than you found it? What could be more important than asking great questions of yourself and those around you?

"Did I offer peace today? Did I bring a smile to someone's face? Did I say words of healing? Did I let go of my anger and resentment? Did I forgive? Did I love? These are the real questions. I must trust that the little bit of love that I sow now will bear many fruits, here in this world and the life to come."
Henri Nouwen

LIFE

"Life is what you make it. Always has been, always will be."
Eleanor Roosevelt

Q: Are your best days ahead of you, or behind you?

The answer that arises from your soul, without having to think too long on this question, indicates much about your view of life. This answer bubbles up from the operating system that has been formed in you over the years through countless decisions and numerous circumstances. Here's the good news, you can change your operating system! Learning how to ask the right questions at the right time can reshape your thoughts, emotions and behaviors. This "Life" section involves the way you look at yourself, those around you

1

and the way you process life's joys and sorrows. Asking great questions about your thoughts of and attitudes towards life will enable you to live life Right Side Up!

> *"Life is not a problem to be solved, but*
> *a reality to be experienced."*
> Soren Kierkegaard

Perspective

Do you look at people and situations like a like a light switch or a dimmer switch? Looking at life as a light switch with two settings, on/off, forces you to view people and yourself on the ends of the spectrum. You and others are either good or bad, you will experience either pleasure/pain, etc. This perspective isn't helpful. Neither you nor your circumstances are as good or bad as you usually perceive them to be. The other option, looking at life as it were a dimmer switch, sees life on a continuum of good, better and best. Looking for the positive qualities in people and situations fosters and environment where you can start from "good," and make steps towards "better," and eventually experience the "best!" Next level living requires embracing healthy and accurate perspectives. How would your reality change if you began to look at life through the lens of good, better, and best?

GOOD   BETTER   BEST

"Between stimulus and response there is a space. In that space is our power to choose our response. In our response lies our growth and our freedom."
Viktor E. Frankl

Q: Does life have to be perfect to be wonderful?

This question flowed from a heart-stirring quote uttered years ago by a man who had lost his teenage daughter in a soul-wrenching auto accident a month earlier. Fighting through his grief and sadness, a moment of perspective burst from his mouth, "Life doesn't have to be perfect to be wonderful." This man grabbed on to hope and health with two fists and held tight! At one of the most painful crossroads of his life he was able to see something bigger, deeper and wider, choosing a healthy mindset rather than simply and painfully wallowing in emotional indulgence. Learning how to properly align your expectations for this life, as well as seeing hope and beauty through the challenges, will enable you to a live life Right Side Up!

"If you think of this world as a place simply intended for our happiness, you find it quite intolerable: think of it as a place for training and correction and it's not so bad."
C.S. Lewis

Q: Am I living out a Fear Story or a Faith Story?

There are two stories you can move towards each day. Two options, two journeys with two different destinations. One is a fear story filled with boogie men and bumps in the night; it is a story where you face insurmountable odds and certain dire consequences at the end of the road. The other side is a faith story– a God written script filled with challenges, hope and triumph at the end of an adventurous journey. If you find yourself anticipating a fear story: Stop, acknowledge the fear story and choose to focus on and live out the wonderful faith story God has called you towards! Are you willing to discover and strive to live out a magnificent faith story?

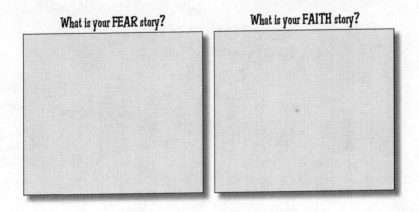

What is your FEAR story?   **What is your FAITH story?**

"Before you attempt to set things right,
make sure you see things right."
John C. Maxwell

Q: What is the most important thing I can do today?

Merely asking this question creates space for you to make a great choice with your day. This is a fantastic question because it allows you to tie heaven and earth together under one bow. The most important thing you can do today may be the smallest or seemingly most insignificant action or activity. Yet, it could be the key, critical path to a fantastic today and a marvelous tomorrow. Asking this great question enables you to grasp the big picture of your life, who you are and what you are called to do. Bringing this question down to the practical level of your daily activities is a big step towards truly living a great life!

"If you read history you will find that the Christians who did most for the present world were just those who thought most of the next...Aim at Heaven and you will get earth 'thrown in,' aim at earth and you will get neither."
C.S. Lewis

Physical Health

How we look, the clothes we wear and the size of our waistline, is far too important to most. Learning how to assign the right value to these issues, to hold these opinions with the right proportion or emphasis is vital for a great life. If we're not careful, these things can move from a *means to an end* and become *an end in themselves*! Is the care we are taking of our physical bodies better or worse than the time and attention we would give our neighbor's pet when they are on vacation? A pet needs, food, water and exercise–and so do you!

"Lack of activity destroys the good condition of every human being, while movement and methodical physical exercise save it and preserve it."
Plato

Q: Where am I experiencing REST?

Neurological studies demonstrate that the brain repairs itself when we sleep. Marketplace research concludes that we will be will be more productive working forty hours a week than ninety. And yet, we keep running and running, mostly on an empty tank. Are you are working for, striving towards and pursuing something that will never provide you the rest your souls craves? It takes discipline to sleep, to play and to rest. The concept of a Sabbath rest has largely been lost in our society and it desperately needs to be brought back. When was the last time you felt refreshed in your soul?

"Rest time is not waste time. It is economy to gather fresh strength... It is wisdom to take occasional furlough. In the long run, we shall do more by sometimes doing less."
Charles Spurgeon

Q: What am I doing for FUEL?

A friend of mine was diagnosed with cancer. He radically changed his eating habits and his body began to fight the cancer to the point where surgery wasn't necessary any more. Don't get me wrong, I know that food isn't magical. But it is true that what you put into your body to nourish and empower you will greatly affect the functionality you will experience throughout the day. What fuel is going into your body?

"Noting tastes as good as healthy feels."
Source Unknown

Q: What am I doing for MOVEMENT?

Scientists studying body mechanics concluded that the body was designed most specifically to run. Long legs, an arched foot, strong lower extremity joints which all form as shock absorbers, pointing to the fact that you were born to run. I hope you enjoy it– I hate it. My body hurts when I run. And yet, I need movement, physical exercise to help all of me—my heart, soul, mind and body, to work at their best. In the old days, physical activity was built into the culture, walking to get water, food or to travel to the next town. Today, discipline is necessary to get the physical activity your body needs. What is your next step in becoming more physically healthy?

"If we could give every individual the right amount of nourishment and exercise, not too little and not too much, we would have found the safest way to health."
Hippocrates

Emotional Health

Many of us marvel at the beautiful complexity of God's design of the human body and how it works. So why does it seem as if people don't look at emotions in the same light? Why can't emotions be viewed as good gifts from God as well? The best amongst us are neither afraid of nor controlled by emotions. Emotions are natural, healthy and enable you to live life according to God's glorious design. They need to be understood, corralled and disciplined to play the role for which they were intended. One of the first steps in fostering emotional health is taking responsibility for your feelings. It is a beautiful moment when we stop blaming people for the past hurts and stop holding people hostage in the present to meet all of our emotional needs.

"My feelings are not God. God is God. My feelings do not define truth. God's word defines truth. My feelings are echoes and responses to what my mind perceives. And sometimes, many times, my feelings are out of sync with the truth. When that happens, and it happens every day in some measure, I try not to bend the truth to justify my imperfect feelings, but rather, I plead with God: Purify my perceptions of your truth and transform my feelings so that they are in sync with the truth."
John Piper

Q: What can I do to feel emotionally full?

There are many unique and wonderful ways to fill your emotional tank. Sitting by a glowing fireplace with a wonderful book, taking a long walk with a trusted friend, or just a few moments of silence in a place of solitude can pour life into your emotional tank. What makes you feel more alive, ready to serve and to be the person God created you to be? Great lives are lived by people who are able to take responsibility for their own emotional health and take proactive steps to make sure their tanks are full!

> "We must have some room to breathe. We need freedom to think and permission to heal. Our relationships are being starved to death by velocity. No one has the time to listen, let alone love. Our children lay wounded on the ground, run over by our high-speed good intentions. Is God now pro-exhaustion? Doesn't He lead people beside the still waters anymore? Who plundered those wide-open spaces of the past, and how can we get them back? There are no fallow lands for our emotions to lie down and rest in."
> Richard Swenson

Q: What would a healthy adult do with this feeling?

Your imagination can be a powerful ally or a crippling enemy. Your greatest hopes and fears come from your imagination. Conversely, you can benefit from your imagination by forming a mental picture of a healthy adult moving through this life. Getting cut off on the freeway, having a friend gossip about you, seeing a letter from the IRS in your mail box, experiencing betrayal or loss can all evoke powerful feelings. No one is perfect, you are human, and picturing how a healthy person would react in certain circumstances can allow you to move towards health and vitality.

"I believe that imagination is stronger than knowledge. The myth is more potent than history. That dreams are more powerful than facts. That hope always triumphs over experience. That laughter is the only cure for grief. And I believe that love is stronger than death."
Robert Fulghum

Q: How can I plug the holes in my emotional tank?

The inevitable hurts and wounds that arise from living life in a broken world poke holes in your emotional tank. Everyone needs healing. Have you ever wondered why such a small comment or action can send you into such an emotional tailspin? You have holes. I have holes. Using the patch kit to repair your emotional holes is an indispensable part of living life Right Side Up. God has given you relationships. Who can you call to help move you towards wholeness? He has also blessed you with wisdom and His Son to carve out a new way of thinking, feeling and relating. Healthy people ask great questions on their way to plugging the holes of their emotional tank! What is the next step in your journey towards healing?

"When we honestly ask ourselves which person in our lives mean the most to us, we often find that it is those who, instead of giving advice, solutions, or cures, have chosen rather to share our pain and touch our wounds with a warm and tender hand."

Henri Nouwen

Decision Making

Peter Drucker says, "Making good decisions is a crucial skill at every level." The ability to collect options, weigh them and make good decisions seems simple. It becomes a little more complex when you begin to analyze whether or not you are going to make the decision in your head, heart, or both. Research on the topic of decision making reveals that many criteria are needed to make great decisions. Like a symphony, good decisions are a melodious blending of your reason, your own experiences, history, the testimony of others and introspective faculty (a fancy way of describing your feelings, and how a decision sits in your heart). The ability to acquire wisdom and make great decisions will be determined by the questions you ask through the process.

> "Learn from yesterday, live for today, hope for tomorrow.
> The important thing is not to stop questioning."
> Albert Einstein

Q: What are my non-negotiables and what are my desires?

The age old skill of comparing pros and cons may be helpful, and it may also be the worst thing you can do to make a good decision. You may actually be comparing a list of positive and negative aspects for two options that shouldn't even be considered as options! Making a list of what you <u>must have</u>, your non-negotiables and your desires–what you <u>would like to have</u>, will enable you to clarify what is most important and foster great decisions. Your best life will be lived when you continually identify and live out the non-negotiables for a Right Side Up life!

> *"It is the nature, and the advantage, of strong people that they can bring out the crucial questions and form a clear opinion about them. The weak always have to decide between alternatives that are not their own."*
> Deitrich Bonhoeffer

Q: What would I tell someone else to do?

Why does it seem that your best advice is freely dished out to others but seldom applied to yourself? The best life seems so clear when we are looking at someone else's life. Discerning people have the ability to become their own life coach. They are aware of the great advice they are giving others and possess the courage and insight to apply it to themselves. This skill will enable you to thrive in your life and relationships. What is the best counsel you've ever given someone? Are you striving to live out those words of wisdom in your own life?

> *"When your values are clear to you, making decisions becomes easier."*
> Roy E. Disney

Q: What evidence would I look for to determine if I made a good decision or not?

Feelings? Outcomes? If you don't know how to look back, reflect and examine if a decision was good or not, you will be blown and tossed by the wind of circumstances and feelings the rest of your life. Establishing clear criteria to evaluate the success of your decision based on a previously identified grid will allow you to increasingly make better decisions. Learning from your past decisions, for better or for worse, allows you to celebrate the good choices and learn from the ones which were not as good. How will you know if this was a good decision or not?

"We have to keep asking ourselves:
'What does it all mean?
What is God trying to tell us? How are we
called to live in the midst of all this?'
Without such questions our lives become numb and flat."
Henri Nouwen

Identity

"I 'm an idiot!" you think to yourself. "I'm a genius!" you might conclude. Your identity is simply who you think you are. Messages from inside your heart and mind are combined with the themes from your outside world to make up your identity. Healthy people have a proactive say in shaping their view of themselves. They have taken control of the messages sent and received to accurately shape who they truly are. The journey towards health includes the ability to identify where you are crafting your identity and learn how to shift your view of yourself to the healthiest and most accurate sources possible!

"Your circumstances won't destroy you, your character will. The things that happen to us don't have nearly the power to undermine our lives as our pride, jealousy, and selfishness do."
Tim Keller

Q: What am I spinning about? (Or where am I building a case?)

Thinking, day dreaming, reflecting, pondering–call it what you will, the people and circumstances your mind drifts to when it is unoccupied points to some of the main sources of your identity. For better or for worse, deeper questions reveal the object you are trusting for the core understanding of your existence. A great question like, "What am I trusting to bring me success, significance and security?" will lead you to the clarity of the hope and the host of your identity. What do you think about when you don't have to think about anything?

"Your religion is what you do with your solitude."
William Temple

Q: What should my identity be based upon?

"Who am I?" may not be a question you've asked yourself or even consciously thought about, but it's a question that you answer every day with the way you live. A target is needed at which to aim. Since God created you (Psalm 139:13), redeemed you (Ephesians 1:7) and loves you like no other (I John 3:1), doesn't it make sense to allow Him to fashion and shape your identity? Listen to the fact that He has made you in His image (Genesis 3), loves you deeply (I John 4) and has sought after you like you were the only one to be found (Jeremiah 31:3)! Are you trusting in what God says about you or not?

"He has great tranquility of heart who cares neither for the praises nor the fault-finding of men. He will easily be content and pacified, whose conscience is pure. You are not holier if you are praised, nor the more worthless if you are found fault with. What you are, that you are; neither by word can you be made greater than what you are in the sight of God."
Thomas a Kempis

Q: How can I shift my identity to something healthier?

What does the process look like to transfer our identity from unhealthy things to God beliefs? Unfortunately discipline alone can't transform our life if we have the wrong captain sailing the ship of our heart/soul. Working in a church years ago I gave everyone a bookmark with a list of our identity in Christ. I decided to review it daily until I believed it. After weeks of trying to convince myself, a question popped into my mind, "If this is true–why do I have to convince myself of it? I don't have to remind myself that I'm a son or a husband–I just am." I decided to quiet myself, ask God to tell me who I am, and wait for His answer. It took a few weeks, but it finally came. God spoke to me, affirming the messages about me He had already declared in the Bible! What a tremendous moment. Love, God's Love, is what will really bring a metamorphosis of our heart and soul!

"Jesus came to announce to us that an identity based on success, popularity and power is a false identity- an illusion! Loudly and clearly he says: 'You are not what the world makes you; but you are children of God."
Henri Nouwen

Purpose

What if the purpose you are living out right now isn't your true purpose? Humans have a crazy knack of grabbing shadow missions and embracing things that are neither good nor healthy. What is your current relationship with your purpose? There are three options pertaining to your purpose; you are either looking for it, living it out, or running from it. Unfortunately, a vision for your life doesn't crawl out from between the stale edges of a fortune cookie, but rather is often wrestled away from the jaws of strife and challenge. If you have been given a purpose from God, especially for you, does it really matter what it is? Does it matter how big or small, how eye catching or obscure your purpose may be? Does life get better the closer you get to living out your intended purpose?

"You are not here merely to make a living. You are here in order to enable the world to live more amply, with greater vision, with a finer spirit of hope and achievement. You are here to enrich the world, and you impoverish yourself if you forget the errand."
Woodrow Wilson

Q: What unique contribution does God want me to make to the world around me?

If you've ever said to yourself, "I was made for this," it is likely that you had a taste of that for which you were designed. Purpose is your higher calling, a noble pursuit and a goal for which you must move towards. When walking through life according to your purpose—you will feel alive and free. Even in the face of significant obstacles, you must align yourself according your unique design, giftedness, passion, calling and character. Do you have a purpose big enough for which you can give your life?

"You have not lived today until you have done
something for someone who can never repay you."
John Bunyan

Q: Is it possible that I'm looking for confirmation of my purpose in the wrong way?

A time out in life is needed. A pause, long enough to look at the signs and symbols for an indication that you are heading in the right direction. To what will you look for a sense of value and validation? Will you look to others for knowing nods of approval and with accompanying feelings of admiration and respect? Is it possible to be right where God wants you to be and yet remain in a very challenging circumstance, void of warm fuzzies? Where you look for your purpose report card will likely determine what you will do with your hours and days.

"The purpose of life is not to be happy. It is to be useful,
to be honorable, to be compassionate, to have it make
some difference that you have lived and lived well."
Ralph Waldo Emerson

Q: Do I understand that I've been loved for a purpose?

Inspiration comes in many forms—a walk in nature, the birth of a child, the beautiful sound of a symphony or a moment of courage in a movie. A compelling story in the Bible about two sons who both missed the heart of their father should remind us about the connection between our belovedness and our purpose. One son ran away, one stayed home (Luke 15). Both missed the reason they were made because they didn't grasp the width and breadth of the Father's love for them. The same is true for us. We will never fully engage in the purpose that God has for us until we fully embrace the amazing and sacrificial love God has for us!

"God's definition of what matters is pretty straightforward. He measures our lives by how we love."
Francis Chan

Happiness/Joy

I f the answer is, "Happiness," then the question is how do we get there? Everyone wants to be happy, but what does it look like and what road does the pursuit of happiness take us down? I taught at a high school a number of years ago. I asked a simple question of the students, "Are you happy?"

90% of Freshmen said, "Yes."

70% of Sophomores said, "Yes."

50% of Juniors said, "Yes."

35% of Seniors said, "Yes."

What is the explanation of this disturbing pattern? Why does happiness trend downward over time for most people? Is it possible to be one of those jovial, grey haired senior citizens who brightens the world with their joy and smile? Can we take active steps to become happier, more joy filled people?

"Let no one ever come to you without leaving better and happier."
Mother Teresa

Q: Am I seeking happiness or joy?

Immanuel Kant shared that there are three things required for happiness: you need to find something to do, someone to love, and something to hope for. What you desire, happiness or joy, impacts the steps on your journey. The pursuit will take you down one road or another depending on whether your quest is for happiness or for joy. Are you looking for a feeling, or a state of being? Through the ages, the pursuit of happiness has been understood to be based on one's circumstances whereas joy seems to be a deeper, more soul involved endeavor. In your life, are you seeking happiness or joy?

"Happiness is like a butterfly; the more you chase it, the more it will elude you, but if you turn your attention to other things, it will come and sit softly on your shoulder."
Henry David Thoreau

Q: Can happiness/joy be achieved directly or is it the result of seeking something else?

A cartoon with two kids talking, accurately summarized the mindset of our culture: One boy says to another, "Money can't buy happiness." The other boy responds, "That's right. Money buys things–and the things make you happy!" Happiness and joy are the result of pursuing something else. They are the by product of conscious decisions to seek something else. What do we need to pursue in order to reap the fruit of happiness/joy as the result?

"Desire that your life count for something great! Long for your life to have eternal significance. Want this! Don't coast through life without a passion."
John Piper

Q: How much of my joy is the result of bringing it to others?

Do you receive joy when you share joy? It seems as if there are two keys to joy: gratitude and generosity. Joyful people are thankful, giving people.

How much delight is there in a parent's heart who toils and labors, serving and leading his child, to be rewarded by the, "proof in the pudding," smile that may be seen in the eyes and on the face of that child? When you seek the joy of those around you, your joy cup begins to fill up and overflow. Whose joy can you work for today?

"Those who are not looking for happiness are the most likely to find it, because those who are searching, forget that the surest way to be happy is to seek happiness for others."
Martin Luther King, Jr.

Shame

I f you have the symptoms, do you have the disease? Few people are courageous enough to admit that they wrestle with shame. Yet, many people wage war on a daily basis with perfectionism, feelings of inferiority, isolation, anger, sadness, the desire to control others and their circumstances, etc. In a word—shame. Shame is both a horrible feeling and a valuable indicator, lighting the road towards health. Your shame can be overcome and healed. How great would it be to live a life free from the shackles of shame?

"Shame is when you feel like a glob of not goodenoughness."
Lewis Smedes

Q: With whom can I be the real me?

There is an interrelatedness, an intimate connection between vulnerability and safety. Many present a pretend self, unwilling to be their genuine selves because they've lived for too long with the message, "If people really knew me—they wouldn't love me." The precious few healthy ones are those who are able to create safe environments, share vulnerably of themselves and are rich in deep relationships. Shame is quelled when we are able to be our true selves, still loved, overcoming the paralyzing fears of rejection and abandonment. But it requires the risk of vulnerability! Are we willing to press past fear and risk the vulnerability of being our true selves with trusted friends?

"To love at all is to be vulnerable. Love anything and your heart will be wrung and possibly broken. If you want to make sure of keeping it intact you must give it to no one, not even an animal. Wrap it carefully round with hobbies and little luxuries; avoid all entanglements. Lock it up safe in the casket or coffin of your selfishness. But in that casket, safe, dark, motionless, airless, it will change. It will not be broken; it will become unbreakable, impenetrable, irredeemable. To love is to be vulnerable."

C.S. Lewis

Q: Which voices am I giving access to my heart and soul?

You are bombarded, daily, with messages telling you what to eat, wear, do and how to evaluate yourself as a person. Sadly, the advertising agencies are winning the battle and most people are defining themselves based on what they have and do versus who they are. Asking great questions affords the opportunity to choose which voices will define you. Regardless of the one you select—the world's, my own, or God's—the voice you listen to will sit on the judgment seat in your heart. The voice you listen to will ultimately determine the source of where you will receive your worth and love. What voice does the, "Healthy you," need to listen to?

*"Our failure to hear His voice when we want to is due
to the fact that we do not in general want to hear it,
that we want it only when we think we need it."*
Dallas Willard

Q: What relationships can help me to heal from shame?

"I'm not really looking for a long term relationship here. Just tell me what books I need to read and I'll be on my way." These were my words, spoken to a wise and insightful counselor. Can you hear the shame dripping from these words? If you are wired like I am, you want healing to be an independent study project that doesn't require other people. I have been haunted by great questions, like this one: "If relationships *helped to cause* my problems, is it possible that relationships are necessary to *help heal* those problems?" This world has been designed to require relationships for healing, which is a beautiful and scary thing. Who has God brought into your life to help you heal?

*"If you put shame in a Petri dish, it needs three things
to grow exponentially: secrecy, silence and judgment. If
you put the same amount of shame in a Petri dish and
douse it with empathy, it can't survive. The two most
powerful words when we're in struggle: me too."*
Brene Brown

Finances

My heart skips a beat every time my wife approaches me with sad and concerned eyes, gently asking, "Which bills would you like me to pay?" Questions like these, questions about money have tormented my soul. Money has many traps. Making, spending, hoarding, and fighting over it, there is good reason for the time and ink the Bible dedicates to address a topic which has taken many hearts hostage. Contrary to popular belief, money isn't the root of all evil, the love of money is (I Timothy 6:10). It is possible to have a healthy view of money, and to discover and live out a beautiful life of contentment (Philippians 4:11-13). How much better would a life be with a healthy view of finances?

"Wise people know that all their money belongs to God and should be used to show that God, and not money, is their treasure, their comfort, their joy, and their security."
John Piper

Q: Am I the owner or the manager?

"Mine!" isn't a cry that kids have to be taught. It is in the nature of people to be possessive. Sharing has to be taught. If we believe in God, then He created everything and it belongs to Him (Psalm 24:1). Being a good administrator of the financial blessings God has given us means living with values that are counter-cultural. How closely are our lives aligned with the financial values of the world? How open are our eyes to seeing and investing God's money according to His values?

"Stewardship is NOT ordering your life in such a way that you can spend money however you want. It's ordering your life in such a way that God can spend YOU in whatever way HE wants."
Chuck Bentley

Q: Have I learned the secret of contentment?

What word first comes to mind when you think of contentment? The path to contentment involves two movements–shifting the object of desire and gratitude. In an age of entitlement, many believe they deserve far better than they ever receive. I know a pastor who will give to anyone who asks of him for two reasons: 1) Because that's what the Bible says; 2) Because it is his declaration that money doesn't have a stranglehold on him. When your heart is at rest with your attitudes and actions involving money, many things are good. Maybe this is why Jesus spent so much time taking about money. Maybe He loves you enough to be concerned with one of the main idols of your heart. Are you able to say, "I don't need that–I'm happy with what I have!" with a pure heart?

"He who is not contented with what he has, would not be contented with what he would like to have."
Socrates

Q: Who can I bless today?

For some, generosity is a life-giving spring that makes them feel alive. But for the majority of the population, giving is difficult because trust is rare. There is an intimate connection between generosity and trust. Do you really have faith that God will take care of your needs? Have you ever blessed someone financially? Why is that occurrence so rare? Those of you who have blessed someone or an organization will agree with me that you probably received more than the recipient. When you take a step of faith with your finances, another step of blessing others comes shortly thereafter. This generosity is seen not only by God but by people. You will become more attractive at work, at home, in marriage and friendship as you fight off a spirit of fear and walk by faith. Where is God calling you to overflow with generosity?

"Do you not know that God entrusted you with that money (all above what buys necessities for your families) to feed the hungry, to clothe the naked, to help the stranger, the widow, the fatherless; and, indeed, as far as it will go, to relieve the wants of all mankind? How can you, how dare you, defraud the Lord, by applying it to any other purpose?"
John Wesley

RELATIONSHIPS

I f you ask people about the best day and the worst day of their lives, there will likely be a single common denominator–people. If you care enough to listen, you will hear stories of how relationships brought them joy & happiness. If you are courageous enough to enter into someone's pain by listening with your heart, you will also hear stories of damaging relationships which ushered sadness & pain into their life.

If you are *wounded in* relationships–is it just possible that healing needs to come *through* relationships? *Yes, full circle.*

Relationships are a powerful instrument–for good or for evil. One man I relationally coached had a horrible marriage, disrupted relationships with his kids and was out of work. After walking together for a while and hearing his story I formulated some great questions to help him navigate into smoother, more peaceful waters. After learning how to pause and ask himself these great questions on a regular basis, he acquired the skill of listening to his wife and caring for her emotions. He also learned how to connect better with his kids. In time, his life's operating system changed to the point where he believed in himself enough to land and keep a great job in order to support his family. A whole beautiful world of satisfying and healthy relationships is available to you if you learn how to walk through this life with great questions! Are you ready for your relationships to be Right Side Up?

"It is my daily mood that makes the weather. I possess tremendous power to make life miserable or joyous. I can be a tool of torture or an instrument of inspiration, I can humiliate or humor, hurt or heal. In all situations, it is my response that decides whether a crisis is escalated or de-escalated, and a person is humanized or de-humanized. If we treat people as they are, we make them worse. If we treat people as they ought to be, we help them become what they are capable of becoming."

J. W. Goethe

Friendship

Considered by some a luxury, friendship is an indispensable part of living a great life. The development of healthy friendships is both an art and a science. Foundationally, friendship needs two components: *discovery* and *development*. If friendships are healthy, they will require work, nurturing and patience. Like a seed planted in the garden, with proper care, something beautiful can happen! Do you believe great friendships are possible in your life?

> *"There is nothing on this earth more to*
> *be prized than true friendship."*
> Thomas Aquinas

Q: With whom can I experience the healthy giving and receiving of a genuine friendship?

What criteria did you use to choose your present friends? Convenience? Necessity? Intentionality? Selection is vital when it comes to friendship. C.S. Lewis draws our attention to this discovery element of a friendship when he explains, "A friend is one who you spend time with and you say, 'You too? Me too. I thought I was the only one!'" Finding a person of quality is the beginning of what could be a nurturing and fruitful friendship. Those with a storehouse of poor friendships need to work on being wiser and more selective, while others with sky-high standards might need to stop voting people off of their friendship island for the slightest infraction. Experiencing healthy relationships that will support and not ridicule, challenge but not demean, begin with seeking out and discovering the right people.

> *"The friend who can be silent with us in a moment of despair or confusion, who can stay with us in an hour of grief and bereavement, who can tolerate not knowing, not curing, not healing and face with us the reality of our powerlessness, that is a friend who cares."*
> Henri Nouwen

Q: What does a healthy friendship look like?

It wasn't until well into adulthood that I sat across the table from someone I would consider a true friend. I spoke and felt understood. I shared and I experienced acceptance. My honesty was met with loving challenges. There are many components to a meaningful and satisfying friendship. Here are a few:

> *Humility*– the courage to be you and to not always have to be right.
> *Acceptance*–admitting the frailty of humanity and being ok with it.
> *Sacrifice*–doing what's best for someone regardless of the cost.

Great friendships ask great questions that identify a clear image of what healthy companionship looks like.

"The beginning of love is to let those we love be perfectly themselves, and not to twist them to fit our own image. Otherwise we love only the reflection of ourselves we find in them."
Thomas Merton

Q: Am I willing to put in the effort necessary to be the friend that I'd like others to be to me?

Meaningful friendships need to be found and forged. There is a cost to mutually satisfying relationships. Everything that is important in life takes work. Work takes work, play takes work and friendships take work. When you deposit the investment of time, vulnerability, emotional & intellectual energy into the right person, a nurturing, challenging and satisfying relationship can emerge. What is your next step in growing a flourishing friendship?

"Have patience with all things, but chiefly have patience with yourself. Do not lose courage in considering your own imperfections but instantly set about remedying them -- every day begin the task anew."
Saint Francis de Sales

Communication

Impactful conversations are a delicate balance between listening and speaking. Great conversationalists care deeply for people. They take the time to craft their words, listen carefully to infer meaning beyond the words spoken, and ultimately create an environment where even in a simple conversation people can feel alive. "The tongue has the power of life and death" (Proverbs 18:21). Healthy communication has the power to not only to exchange information but to actually leave another individual (and the relationship) healthier than before the conversation began. Communicating well can help us to embrace life Right Side Up!

> *"I've learned that people will forget what you said,*
> *people will forget what you did, but people will*
> *never forget how you made them feel."*
> Maya Angelou

Q: Am I willing to let the other person be the hero of our conversation?

Conversation heroes are humble, giving others room to talk, setting them up for success with the goal of a relational win–not a conversation victory. These people ask questions, stop and listen to responses with both their ears and their heart. This gift enables those around them the freedom, space and enjoyment of self-discovering life changing truths. Do you need to be the hero of the conversation or can you let those around you experience the joy of learning by self-discovery? How good are you at asking questions and allowing others to find their way?

"Do not imagine that if you meet a really humble man he will be what most people call 'humble' nowadays: he will not be a sort of greasy, smarmy person, who is always telling you that, of course, he is nobody. Probably all you will think about him is that he seemed a cheerful, intelligent chap who took a real interest in what you said to him. If you do dislike him it will be because you feel a little envious of anyone who seems to enjoy life so easily. He will not be thinking about humility: he will not be thinking about himself at all."
C.S. Lewis

Q: Can I build a bridge for understanding?

There is a word for identifying with another person's situation–empathy, which means *to feel with*. It isn't necessary for empathy to have experienced the exact same circumstances as another. What is essential is that you can relate their feelings to your own story. In the course of a conversation, or series of conversations, you may discover that you don't understand why someone feels the way they do. But, even if you don't understand why they feel that way, you can identify and empathize with those same feelings in your own life. You may not be able to relate to that particular temptation, but you can relate to feelings of temptation in other areas of your life. Identifying and relating their feelings to your own builds a bridge of understanding between the two of you, diminishing judgment and transforming a small conversation into a life giving salve. How much time, effort or energy are you putting into empathy?

"If we are to love our neighbors, before doing anything else we must see our neighbors. With our imagination as well as our eyes, that is to say like artists, we must see not just their faces but the life behind and within their faces. Here it is love that is the frame we see them in."
Frederick Buechner

Q: Can I communicate in such a way that others understand me?

Have you ever noticed that you can communicate clearly in one context but find it difficult to communicate in another? What makes conversation so easy with a co-worker, but so difficult with a friend or loved one? Saying what you mean in a way that can be understood is not always as easy as it sounds. The burden of clear communication rests largely on the speaker. If you can communicate clearly in one arena, be encouraged! If you can communicate with clarity in one set of relationships, you only need to learn how to do so in the important conversations with loved ones who matter most. Great conversationalists speak simply, plainly and directly without clouding or obscuring their message. Healthy communicators pair the right information with the right emotions—conveyed through tone, word choice, or body language—enabling those who hear to better understand the words and the heart behind them. How clearly are you communicating your thoughts and emotions to those around you?

> "Speak clearly, if you speak at all; carve
> every word before you let it fall."
> Oliver Wendell Holmes, Sr.

Connection

Connection is a "We" sport. Despite the fact that most of us go through life surrounded by people, "We" is a difficult concept for many to grasp. Western society, broken families and rugged individualism has fostered an environment that elevates the individual and is suspect or even hostile to the concept of togetherness. "We" requires dependence on others–fallible people who may let us down. Some will ask themselves, "Am I getting what I need in this relationship? Does she complete me? Am I being heard, valued, and understood?" These questions can lead to becoming a "Me Monster" (see Brian Regan for an example). Something as simple as shifting the pronouns in our life from, "I," or "Me," to "We," can be a helpful, concrete step in connecting in our most important relationships!

> *"Life is relationships–the rest is just details."*
> Gary Smalley

Q: Am I connected to my own heart?

"Do you have this same challenge connecting with other people? Who have you connected best with during the course of your life?" These questions I've asked of those I coach to reveal a simple and shocking truth–many can't connect with others because they are disconnected from themselves. Hurt, abuse and unhealed wounds can make you shrink back from relationships, and in fact, disconnect from your own heart. Reconnecting with your heart often means walking down a road of healing past hurts, learning to relate to others in a heathy way, opening yourself up to feel again—to live and to be fully alive!

"Because true belonging only happens when we present our authentic, imperfect selves to the world, our sense of belonging can never be greater than our level of self-acceptance."
Brene Brown

Q: Have I created an environment conducive for connection?

Relationships have weather systems. Some are cold and rainy while others are warm and sunny. The safety you give to others, to be and to share themselves, allows for the true vulnerability necessary for connection. A safe environment allows for authenticity and honesty which creates the space needed for slow, consistent and beautiful relational growth. Safety is of paramount importance when it comes to connecting. Identifying how much of your true self you are bringing to a relationship will be a great indicator of your connectedness and satisfaction with that relationship. How well are you building a safe environment for connection?

"Vulnerability is the birthplace of connection and the path to the feeling of worthiness. If it doesn't feel vulnerable, the sharing is probably not constructive."
Brene Brown

Q: Am I striving to meet others needs according to design?

"All of them," and, "None of them," are both wrong answers to the same question, "What needs of theirs am I designed to meet?" Meeting the needs of another person is at the heart of genuine connection. People have different needs. You are created to meet either a general or specific need in a person's life. For connection to thrive, effort needs to be put forth to discover and satisfy the needs for which you were designed to meet—no more and no less. How hard are you working to meet the greatest needs of the people whom you love?

"Piglet sidled up to Pooh from behind. "Pooh?" he whispered.
"Yes, Piglet?"
"Nothing," said Piglet, taking Pooh's hand.
"I just wanted to be sure of you."
A.A. Milne, *Winnie-the-Pooh*

Conflict Resolution

Tension infiltrates most relationships. The health of a relationship can generally be evaluated by the frequency and duration of conflict in a relationship. Healthy people acknowledge that conflict is an inevitable and necessary part of a relationship. For those who fail to ask great questions, disagreements, arguments and relational struggles are more like trains than planes. Like a train, their troubles follow discernable and predictable tracks, repeated patterns of pulling people near, pushing them away and either stuffing or venting their emotions. Conversely, when we notice and acknowledge what patterns are present in a conflict and why they are there, we jump off of the tracks leading us towards a predictable destination and embrace the freedom of flying to new heights of healthier conflict resolution. Those who want to live Right Side Up will ask the questions necessary to turn tension and turmoil into transparency and tranquility.

> *"Intimacy equals resolved conflict."*
> Howard Hendricks

Q: Is it possible that I am wrong?

"He may not always be right, but he's never in doubt." This funny phrase is the one we use in our house about those who have too much pride for a healthy dialogue. For most, winning an argument is important—too important. If you are willing to be humble, conceding a valid point, leaving room for error when there is ambiguity, margin will be created in your relationships that will lower the frequency and intensity of your conflicts. Are you willing to leave some space for the possibility of being wrong?

"It was pride that changed angels into devils; it is humility that makes men as angels."
St. Augustine

Q: What do I really want?

Few have paused long enough purposefully declare what is truly desired in a relationship. In absence of this decision, feelings and fleeting moments determine conversational marching orders rather than the ultimate goal of the relationship. Mature and discerning people ask destination questions, identifying the possible results a discussion may have on a relationship. Even the question, "Do you want to be right or be happy?" is a good, not great question. This places happiness at the ultimate high spot on the board of achievement. How about, "Do you want to be right or be healthy?" How have you defined the "win" in your relationships? If you want to get on the same side with another person, mutual purpose needs to be identified and moved towards. What do you really want in life and out of your relationships?

"Your feet will bring you to where your heart is."
Irish Proverb

Q: How much have I contributed to this situation?

The ability to step outside of a conflict and assess your contribution, your part in a conflict, ignites a discovery conversation that will shift your sails away from blame and head towards a healthy resolution. Recognizing our contribution involves taking the right amount of responsibility, acknowledging the discernable pattern of your conflicts and being aware of what percentage of your conflict is coming from your past woundedness and what percent is coming from the current tension. Humbly taking ownership over your part may be the key that begins a new, healthy season of more easily resolving conflicts in your relationships.

"The man with insight enough to admit his
limitations comes nearest to perfection."
Johann Wolfgang von Goethe

Single (Singleness)

I f you are single, happy, healthy and don't want to be married, please ignore this section. If you are single and want to be married, you just may find some value in these great questions. In our culture, single people have unique challenges to navigate. If any of us are defined by our marital status or anything other than being made in the image of God, and being deeply loved by Him, we are on shaky ground. As one of my good friends says, "The truest thing about you isn't your marital status—it's the fact that you've been made in the image of God!" The biggest challenge in life is to be rightly defined and rightly connected to God (and to the right people).

"If we seek paradise outside ourselves, we
cannot have paradise in our hearts."
Thomas Merton

Q: How is my past impacting my ability to develop healthy relationships now?

Regardless of whether your pain and injury was a self-inflicted wound or came from another, that pain needs to be addressed or it will continue to be toxic in your present and future relationships. Don't shoot the messenger! Your past relationships and experiences influence, but don't dictate your present reality. Relational pain is like pushing a ball underwater—it will explode up at some point, it's just a matter of where and when. Where do you need to experience health and healing?

"Until you heal your past, your life patterns and relationships will continue to be the same, it's just the faces that change."
B. Grace Jones

Q: What do I believe about marriage?

Do I believe marriage is worth pursuing? Is marriage going to answer all my problems and fulfill all my desires? Do I want to marry? Is marriage God's best for me? These basic questions about the concept of marriage itself can enlighten and inform the single person much about their hearts attitude towards marriage. Your mindset towards, understanding and expectations of marriage create the framework from which you will look for a spouse, maintain relationship and experience connection. Have you really analyzed what you believe about marriage itself?

"Cinderella never asked for a prince. She asked for a night off and a dress."
Kiera Cass

Q: What steps do I need to take to become healthier?

"You basically get the same level of health in a partner that you are currently living." This was the sentiment of one of my single/dating/soon to be married friends. He continued, "Too many of us ask the wrong question: Will the next person make my life great? Will the person provide for me and help me to live out the grand adventure for which I was designed?" He continued, "the better question is: Would I date someone who _____? (Works like me; engages people in relationships like me; exercises like me; uses money like me; etc.). The healthier a person becomes, physically, emotionally, spiritually, in friendships, at work and with family, the easier it becomes for him or her to spot a healthy partner with whom to build a life. God rewards healthy steps. In His way, in His time–He blesses the great questions we ask and the great choices we make.

"Investing in yourself is the best investment you will ever make. It will not only improve your life; it will improve the lives of all those around you."
Robin Sharma

Marriage (Couples)

"*D*id *you love the person I gave you to love?*" There are some who think this question will be asked when we get to Heaven. Maybe it will, maybe it won't. There is an exquisite beauty found in a committed & loving marriage that few have witnessed & even fewer have experienced. Marriage relationships are difficult and require much work. The myth of the easy going soul mate who will complete you is just that—a myth. Work takes work, play takes work and so do relationships. Asking great questions can help create a Right Side Up marriage! What do you think, do people marry amazing people or do people work hard to help each other become amazing? ✓

"A relationship, I think, is like a shark. You know?
It has to constantly move forward or it dies."
Woody Allen

Q: What do I need to CELEBRATE about my spouse?

Many spouses have wonderful qualities that go unnoticed and unappreciated. The Reticular Activating System is the part of the brain that unconsciously looks for supporting evidence for your judgments and beliefs. You can actually retrain your brain to look for, monitor and bring attention to the good qualities, character traits and choices your spouse makes.

Celebrating the great qualities of your spouse/significant other refocuses your heart and mind, enabling you to experience marriage at a higher level. When it comes to your spouse, are you looking for good or are you hyper-focused on the areas that need improvement?

> *"Any fool can walk in off the street and tell*
> *you what's wrong with something.*
> *It takes wisdom to discover what is right*
> *and good about something."*
> Howard Hendricks

Q: When I think of my spouse, for what am I most THANKFUL?

The art of gratitude has a way of shaping and molding your life and relationships like few things can. The ability to be grateful for what you have, without comparing to others, is a beautiful thing indeed! A recent marriage study out of the University of Georgia discovered that appreciating one's spouse was the main key in lasting and loving marriages. Do you know what a hungry heart looks like after it is satisfied? Thankful! Gratitude in a relationship is the continual expression of a desire for and enjoyment of another.

> *"To be grateful is to recognize the love of God in everything."*
> Thomas Merton

Q: How can I BLESS my spouse today?

Would you agree with me that selfishness is the number one problem and greatest threat to a healthy marriage? If this is true, the ability to look past your wants and desires in order to serve will enable you to love and connect with your spouse in a new, fresh and healthy way. It's so sad when the petty woundedness of a relationship launches a downward trajectory that can evolve into a death spiral. The upside down marriage reacts negatively, "I'm not going to _____ because they aren't _____." When you realize that you are blessed to be a blessing, you care about the other's needs above your own and that relationship will find its rightful place in your heart and in the universe.

"Our real blessings often appear to us in the shape of pains, losses and disappointments; but let us have patience and we soon shall see them in their proper figures."
Joseph Addison

Parenting

P arenting is one of the most rewarding and challenging jobs in this life. I remember being asked a paralyzing question mere days before the birth of my first child: "You are going to have to decide—do you want to be liked or respected?" Ouch! So many parents are trying to be their child's best friend. Children will find friends. What they really need is the love, trust and guidance of a loving parent whom they respect!

"Life affords no greater responsibility, no greater
privilege, than the raising of the next generation."
C. Everett Koop

Q: Do I have a clear vision of the person my child can be?

How will you know if your parenting is working or not? What are you going to point to as evidence that you did a good job raising your child? Many of us know what we don't want our kids to be. Do you know who you want your child to become? Have you communicated this goal to them as well? Picking what is most important in life, including the three character traits you deem most important, and then holding those fast and true, with constant reminders, will set your child up for success in amazing ways. If you want your child to live life Right Side Up, help them to see a beautiful picture of what their life can be!

*"The most pathetic person in the world is someone
who has sight, but has no vision."*
Helen Keller

Q: Am I trusting God with the results? *Yes*

"Parenting is a long series of decisions to let go." These wise words flowed from the mouth of a friend whose children were out of the house living their own productive adult lives. He continued to share from his deep well of experience, "We let go of them as they crawl, walk, ride a bike, go to kindergarten, off to high school, college and then marry." Whoosh! That's parenting in a nutshell and it will drive you crazy if you don't learn how to lean on and trust in God with your child's life. As much as we'd like to, we can't control the end product of who our child will become. Influence–yes. Inspire–yes. Impart–yes. Control–no. The sovereign God of the universe knows better than you how to raise your kids.

*"Don't forget–God can do for your kids
what he has done for you."*
Howard Hendricks

Q: Am I modeling the life that I want my kids to live?

Joy. Peace. Freedom. What would your child's life be like if they regularly saw these characteristics in your life? "Do as I say, not as I do," is not a good parenting strategy. They watch, imitate and live out much of the life they see in you. Your life and character are the most influential factors in shaping your child's current and future life operating system. It is your responsibility to demonstrate for your children a life with a thoughtful perspective on people, a healthy mindset and a fantastic relationship with a powerful and compelling God!

> *"Children have never been very good at listening to their elders, but they have never failed to imitate them."*
> James Baldwin

Y our kids are reading a life-changing book. For better
or worse, this book will shape their future and may
determine the quality of their life for all of their days.
They are reading this book every day. As they read, unexpressed
questions form in their minds but never reach their lips. This
book is YOU! This book is YOUR LIFE. Your influence will
sculpt their character and proactively mold the way they look
at and interact with themselves and the world around them. As
they read the book of your life, your kids are silently asking crucial
questions about you! These wordless dialogues will lay the tracks
that can lead them towards either fulfilling relational connections
or dissatisfying relational detachment. Are you interested in
learning the questions your kids are silently asking of you?

> *"To bring up a child in the way he should go,*
> *travel that way yourself once in a while."*
> Josh Billings

Your kids are silently asking of you…

Q: Can I trust your words and actions?

Typical moments on playgrounds and grocery store aisles
across America sound like this. "Jimmy–no. Put that down.

Jimmy. I said no. Jimmy–NO! Jimmy, I told you not to play with that." Kid cries. Kid whines. Other parents stare. Pause. "Well, you can play with it for just a few minutes." Bam! In a split second, credibility is broken and respect floats away. When our words lose their weightiness, the relationship becomes strained and confidence erodes. Respect is built and maintained when healthy boundaries are set and enforced. If you love your kids, are you willing to be a person of your word? What does your "yes" or "no" actually mean?

> *"You don't always know what your kids will do, but
> your kids should always know what you will do."*
> Joyce Sanders

Your kids are silently asking of you…

Q: Will you love me always and forever?

Guess How Much I Love You by Sam Mc Bratney and Anita Jeram, was one of my favorite books to read to the kids when they were younger. I loved when Big Nut-brown Hair would trump the love expressed by his child, whispering at the end, "I will love you up to the moon–and back." Your child wants to know if your love has limits, if there are borderlines on your loyalty and commitment to them. There are two sides to love, the warm, sensitive caring side and the more challenging tough love side. Neither are easy, both are required. Setting firm boundaries and making difficult choices may be the best way you can possibly love your child as they grow into adulthood. How will you show, not tell, your child that you will love them always and forever–up to the moon and back?

"Intense love does not measure, it just gives."
Mother Teresa

Your kids are silently asking of you…

Q: When will you be proud of me?

"When am I most proud of you?" I asked this probing question one night as I was laying my 7-year-old daughter to bed. She squinted her eyes, thought deeply for a few seconds, smiled as if she caught me in a trap and said, "Now Daddy! You are always proud of me." I'm certainly not a perfect parent, but over the years I have learned the importance of and the steps needed to help my children understand that I am proud of who they are (character) and not just what they do (behavior). Celebrate the great character choices your child makes! Seek any opportunity to validate who he/she is, over what he/she does (or doesn't do.) Champion who your child is becoming and he/she will know that the answer to "When will my mom or dad be proud of me?" is–now and forever… because I love you!

"If you want your children to improve, let them overhear
the nice things you say about them to others."
Haim Ginott

Love

L ove is at the heart of every great story. There is tension, a problem to be solved, a hero beating the odds to rescue someone—and there is love in the center of it all. Your life is a reaction to the love you have either received or have been denied. This powerful, mysterious and sometimes mystifying concept is at the heart of everything for which you long and work. Love frees, emboldens and gives hope for your journey through life. "Faith, hope and love, but the greatest of these is love." I wondered for years why love was the best of these three amazing traits. Then one day, it dawned on me, at the end of it all, in Heaven, there will no longer be need for faith and hope—but love will continue for all of eternity! How beautiful would life be if we cultivated a flourishing love that increased in intensity, growing stronger and wider?

> *"One word frees us of all the weight and*
> *pain of life: That word is love."*
> Sophocles

Q: What is love?

It is in our DNA to keep score in our relationships. True love keeps score of the right things, trying to out serve, out listen and out care for the other. Love as a _principle_ can be seen in I Corinthians 13. There, love is described as being patient, kind, keeping no records of wrong, not being selfish, rejoicing in the truth. Love as a _person_ can be seen in Jesus. He embodied love in its fullness and wrapped a human body around it. Love is not a feeling but an action, a sacrifice for the good of the other. If you want to know what love is, look for someone who seeks the good of others and is willing to sacrifice for them. How well are you loving others right now?

> "I have found the paradox, that if you love until it
> hurts, there can be no more hurt, only more love."
> Mother Teresa

Q: Am I loving the same way I've been loved?

Do I have broken definition of love? Yes. It seems as though we all do. The question is not _if_ we have a broken definition of love, but _how do we fix it?_ Broken understandings of love burst toxically into relationships when we write the wrong answer to this finish the statement, "If they really loved me they would _____.." More often than not, if people "loved us" in the way the unhealthy parts of us want to be loved, that wouldn't be real love. Most people are love mirrors–loving the way they perceive they have been loved, merely reflecting the love they have been shown. We have probably received and are living out a somewhat tweaked understanding of love and passing it on to those around us. On the other hand, a correct understanding of love will go a long way to bless our lives and relationships. The solution is to humbly seek true love for yourself and others. This is a long journey in the right direction. Where is your definition of love warped?

"Love is not only something you feel, it is something you do."
David Wilkerson

Q: How can my love grow?

Being told to love is good. Being shown how to love is better. Being loved is the greatest of all. Sometimes love grows by merely allowing yourself to be loved. People are trying to love you. Are you letting that love in? They see something lovable in you that you may need to recognize in yourself. Will the quality of your life increase with an enlarged capacity to love those around you? If loving and being loved is at the heart of a Right Side Up life, are you willing to risk the uncomfortable transition time to embrace a new, higher, deeper and wider love?

"We have to allow ourselves to be loved by the people who really love us, the people who really matter. Too much of the time, we are blinded by our own pursuits of people to love us, people that don't even matter, while all that time we waste and the people who do love us have to stand on the sidewalk and watch us beg in the streets! It's time to put an end to this. It's time for us to let ourselves be loved."
C. JoyBell C.

SECTION 3

SPIRITUAL LIFE

*W*hat role is God playing in your life right now? Is it possible that your spiritual life is the most important, yet possibly most neglected facet of living a great life? God has designed you with a body, mind, soul and a spirit. Great questions need to be asked and thoughtful energy needs to be put forth to flourish in this life as intended. Your spiritual life is the key to unlocking healing, health and relational vibrancy. Consider the fact that God asked great questions to draw people towards Himself and to a Right Side Up life:

"Where are you?" (Genesis 3:9)
"Should I not be concerned with that great city?" (The Father – Jonah 4:11).

"Do you believe that I am able to do this?" (Jesus – Matthew 9:28).
"Who do you say I am?" (Jesus – Luke 9:20).
"Who will get what you've worked for?" (Jesus – Luke 12:20).
"When the Son of Man comes, will he find faith on the earth?" (Jesus – Luke 18:8).
"Why do you call me good?" (Jesus – Luke 18:19).
"What do you want me to do for you?" (Jesus – Luke 18:41)

God asks buckets of amazing questions to create space for you to self-discover truth, health and life! If you're ready for a Right Side Up life–dive into these questions on a regular basis and prepare to be challenged and blessed!

"The spiritual life is not a life before, after or beyond our everyday existence. No, the spiritual life can only be real when it is lived in the midst of the pains and joys of the here and now."
Henri Nouwen

God

cknowledged or not, God is the beginning, the end and everything in between. In His own words, He has declared himself the, "Alpha and Omega" (Revelation 22:13). Understanding God and your relationship with Him forges the operating system through which you will look at and interact with the world. As A.W. Tozer explains, "We by some secret law of the soul gravitate towards our image of God." Therefore, he concludes, "What we think about God is the most important things about us!" If you become like your God, it is crucial to have an accurate portrait of Him. Is your God a friend or a fiend? Is He compassionate or callous? Is He quick to forgive or mounting bitterness against you? Understanding who God *really* is, not who you think He is and certainly not just a bigger version of you or your parents, is an important key to meaningful relationships and a Right Side Up life.

"My Trust in God flows out of the experience of his loving me, day in and day out, whether the day is stormy or fair, whether I'm sick or in good health, whether I'm in a state of grace or disgrace. He comes to me where I live and loves me as I am."
Brennan Manning

Q: What does God THINK about me right now?

Having asked this question to hundreds of people in my lifetime, I discovered something startling. The vast majority of people shared a single word answer–*Disappointed*. "I think God is disappointed with me," was the dejected response from the vast majority of the people I've asked. Do you want to be with, draw near to, or share a relationship with someone who is constantly disappointed with you? Critical to your prayer life, worship and missional living is an accurate comprehension of what God thinks about you. So what does God think about you right now? Do you have the courage to agree with Him?

> *"Me Abba is very fond of me."*
> Brennan Manning

Q: How do I FEEL in God's presence?

Feelings are supposed to be morally neutral. True. And they are also helpful indicators of your thoughts and perspective of a relationship. Whether it is flat on your face (Numbers 20:6) or approaching the throne of grace with confidence (Hebrews 4:16), identifying the experienced feelings you have in God's presence clarifies your present understanding of Him. Awareness of your feelings in His presence enables you to accurately refine your understanding of who He is. The Bible says that God is both big and near. In this life, it is necessary to walk in the tension of experiencing the awe of the transcendent

God and the closeness of the God who is willing to call you His child and His friend. How do you feel in God's presence?

"Though our feelings come and go, God's love for us does not."
C.S. Lewis

Q: What does God WANT from me?

"What in the world does God want from me?!" A frustrated and curious man who had neither grown up in nor ever attended a church continued his rant to a trusted friend, "What does He want from me? My time? My money? What does God want from me?!" God has both general and specific desires for each of us to fulfill. Spending your time pursuing, discovering and joyfully living out God's desires for your life is worthwhile indeed! So what does God want from you?

"Give me all of you!!! I don't want so much of your time,
so much of your talents and money, and so much of your
work. I want YOU!!! ALL OF YOU!! … Give me yourself
and in exchange I will give you Myself. My will, shall
become your will. My heart, shall become your heart."
C.S. Lewis

Message of Christianity

Regardless of where people are on their spiritual journey, I love to ask them, "What is your understanding of the message of Christianity?" I can begin with what they think Christianity is, celebrate the parts they got right and try to clarify where they may have misunderstood the message Jesus brought. One man shared a common response to my question by saying, "I think Christianity means that if you live a perfect life, like Jesus did, then you'll get to go to Heaven." To his astonishment, I shared with him that I would have never signed up for that deal. He was shocked and amazed when I shared with him a message of love, forgiveness and the sacrifice of another—the true message of the gospel. Tim Keller shares that there are three aspects of the gospel, each of which is important and can't be left out: Historical (the doctrine of what God has done for us), Sonship (how we have a new identity in Christ) and our participation in His Kingdom (where the values of the world are turned upside down). What is your understanding of the message of Christianity?

"Christ did not die to forgive sinners who go on treasuring anything above seeing and savoring God. And people who would be happy in heaven if Christ were not there, will not be there. The gospel is not a way to get people to heaven; it is a way to get people to God. It's a way of overcoming every

obstacle to everlasting joy in God. If we don't want God
above all things, we have not been converted by the gospel."
John Piper

Q: Am I living out a good works gospel or a good news gospel?

Good work is something you do. It is a current pursuit to make yourself fit and presentable. On the contrary, good news is something that has happened—it's in the past. What separates the message of Christianity from every other religion is the loving tenderness of a Father, the sacrifice of a Son, and the grace the Holy Spirit brought you at the beginning and throughout your journey. There is a reason that God refers to your good works in negative, graphic language (Isaiah 64:6 – "filthy rags"). God desires your heart and gratitude. This will never happen if you think you've accomplished the feat of earning your salvation yourself. What is the object of your faith—your performance or Jesus'?

"Jesus Christ lived the life you should have lived, and died
the death you should have died as your substitute in your
place, so that God would receive you not for your record and
for your sake, but for Jesus' record and for Jesus' sake."
Tim Keller

Q: Has my verdict come before my performance? (Thanks Tim Keller for inspiring this question!)

"There is no such thing as a free lunch." "Pull yourself up by your bootstraps." Culture is full of messages encouraging you to be a self-made person, to perform well and to be rewarded for that performance. When it comes to your relationship with God, He bestows upon you a verdict before you begin to "perform." You now have the freedom of a child of God who has been declared loved, forgiven, adopted and an ambassador. You can go through life seeking to do good things, not to earn the favor of the Almighty, but to say, "Thank you!" to a generous Father and a loving Son who was willing to sacrifice Himself for you! Once a coach told his team, "Your teammates love you, your parents love you, your teachers love you and I love you. Go play like you're loved!" God wants *you* to live like you are loved!

> "God does not so much want us to do things
> as to let people see what He can do."
> A.B. Simpson

Q: What is the difference between a pardon and an adoption?

A release from prison, not being justly punished for one's actions is a good thing–but it's not the best thing. An adoption into the loving arms of a parent who chose us and pledged to never let us go is even better! Sadly, there are many in the world of Christianity who think of salvation as *just* a pardon, forgetting that they were also blessed through an amazing adoption, a joy filled relationship intended to satisfy their souls! Are you living as a pardoned criminal or an adopted child?

"If anybody understands God's ardor for his children, it's someone who has rescued an orphan from despair, for that is what God has done for us. God has adopted you. God sought you, found you, signed the papers and took you home."
Max Lucado

Daily

What are the most important questions you could ask yourself everyday? The things we do everyday are important. Eat, sleep, relate to people are all indispensable parts of a basic quality life. Yes, brushing your teeth and using deodorant on a daily basis are important. But, if this life isn't all there is, and your physical body will one day be renewed, asking these three questions below may be *the* most important thing. Below are some foundational questions that if asked daily, will capture your heart and mind and set you on a new course for a beautiful, fruitful and fulfilled life—the Right Side Up life!

> *"It was when I was happiest that I longed most...*
> *The sweetest thing in all my life has been the longing...*
> *to find the place where all the beauty came from."*
> C.S. Lewis

Addressed to God…

Q: What do I need to CELEBRATE about YOU?

A friend of mine, a wonderful man of God, had a battle with cancer—and won! He humbly shared with me from his experience, "Until you've stared death in the face, and have not been afraid because of the trust you have in God, you really don't know how solid your faith is." Drawing your attention towards God, in a movement of celebration directs your thoughts to focus in on what is good and lovely about the God you seek and serve. If Jesus, as your example, spent many mornings in a quiet place connecting with and celebrating the Father, how much more should you?

> *"Without the Way there is no going; without the Truth there is no knowing; without the Life there is no living."*
> Thomas á Kempis

Q: What do I need to REMEMBER about the GOSPEL?

The leaders of the early church sewed their testimony inside their cloaks so they might never forget the marvelous things God had done for them. The gospel, the message of Christianity is the most important thing we can reset on a daily basis. Hebrews 2:1 reminds us that, 'We must pay the most careful attention, therefore, to what we have heard, so that we do not drift away." In order to live out a powerful and compelling gospel, the good news message of Jesus, we need to find ways of preaching the gospel to ourselves everyday! We need to remember that, "While we were yet sinners, Christ died for us" (Romans 5:8).

> *"If you believe what you like in the gospels, and reject what you don't like, it is not the gospel you believe, but yourself."*
> St. Augustine

Q: What do I need to EMBRACE about ETERNITY?

One of my close friends, a humble and godly man, suddenly got cancer and died a few months after his diagnosis. He peacefully shared with me days before his death, "I'm ready to go Home." When you live with your heart and mind set on heavenly things (Colossians 3:1-4), you don't get caught up in the pettiness and pitiful nature of living only for what is seen and temporary (II Corinthians 4:18). Are you living this life as if you really believe that the best is yet to come?

"If you read history you will find that the Christians who did most for the present world were precisely those who thought most of the next. It is since Christians have largely ceased to think of the other world that they have become so ineffective in this."
C.S. Lewis

Journey Home

I f you are on a journey Home towards the Father's heart, you must remember that you have a privilege and a calling to help others to find their way Home as well. Whether you are beckoned, pushed, prodded, responding to a transformed life (Mark 5:1ff) or being obedient to a command (Matthew 28:16-20), if you are connected to God you are putting some thought and effort into helping the people around you to find a relationship with Him. The people you rub shoulders with on a daily basis are asking a series of concentric, deeper questions examining your candidacy as a person worthy of helping them to find their way Home.

"God is not just one thing we add to the mix
called life. He wants an invitation from us to
permeate everything and every part of us."
Francis Chan

Q: Would I like to be your friend?

If you haven't helped the people around you experience acceptance, helped them feel like they belong and have significance, do you really think they will be willing to listen to what you have to say about life, God and eternity? The people around you will never want to hear anything from you if they first haven't decided you are a person worthy of friendship. There is a huge difference between a Christian who is a friend and a friend who is a Christ-follower. If you develop genuine friendships with people, the love and care you show to them may lead them straight to the heart of the Father!

> *"Walking with a friend in the dark is better than walking alone in the light."*
> Helen Keller

Q: Would I like to know your God?

Every day you live, every decision you make, every relationship you have declares what you know to be true about God. That's why faith is so important to God. Faith is the active declaration that God is good, holy, loving and desires to have a relationship with everyone! True faith, lived out well, will breathe joy and peace into an individual's life and relationships. Is the portrait of God you are showing to the world through your life one that is compelling and contagious?

> *"God creates out of nothing. Wonderful you say.*
> *Yes, to be sure, but he does what is still more*
> *wonderful; he makes saints out of sinners."*
> Soren Kierkegaard

Q: Would I like to embrace your gospel?

An accurate understanding of the gospel can allow you to live either a lighter life with more freedom and grace, or a heavier life with burdensome boundary markers. When I first found a true relationship with God, my life was transformed. Forgiven! Now there was peace and joy flowing from my life. But then I stepped in again, telling God, "I'll take it from here." I became the best, most conservative and miserable Pharisee ever! The apostle Paul finally asked me a question that got me back on the grace track, "After beginning with the Spirit, are you now trying to attain your goal by human effort?" (Galatians 3:3). Guilty as charged. The gospel, the message of Christianity you are living out, will either bring freedom, life and grace to yourself and those around you—or a sense of rules and shame for not having lived up to them. Is your gospel Right Side Up?

"If your Gospel isn't touching others, it hasn't touched you!"
Curry R. Blake

Worship

God's first command, "Have no other gods before me," (Exodus 20:1-3) is a warning and encouragement to fill your life with worship of Him. You have a choice, everyday, to either worship God (Matthew 6:9), yourself, or your selfish desires (Philippians 3:19). If you are wise and courageous enough, your worship of God will transform your life and relationships, bringing them into alignment with God's glorious design!

"I can safely say, on the authority of all that is revealed in the Word of God, that any man or woman on this earth who is bored and turned off by worship is not ready for heaven."
A.W. Tozer

Q: Who or what is the object of my worship?

Seldom spoken of, worship is constantly given. Adoration, devotion—worship is that to which you give your attention and affection. Humans are hard wired for worship, designed to praise something or someone. Sadly, many choose to worship their work, family, money, success or people. These objects of worship will never satiate the soul's need nor meet its desire to have something valuable to worship. The pressing question is what, or who, is the *object* of your worship?

"Isn't it a comfort to worship a God we cannot exaggerate?"
Francis Chan

Q: What kind of life is my current worship producing?

In a pragmatic fashion it is wise to ask, "How is it working for you?" Your current object of worship is either bringing you something good or bad. Your worship impacts you individually. Some objects of worship, money, power, prestige have the promise of a fulfilling pay off and leave you empty inside. Your worship will also impact your relationships. For better or worse, your worship is developing a relational operating system that will either bring a wake of goodness and mercy (Psalms 1) or strife (Hosea 10:13).

"There can only be two basic loves...the love of
God unto the forgetfulness of self, or the love of self
unto the forgetfulness and denial of God."
St. Augustine

Q: For what am I expressing thanks?

Worship based in fear is appeasement. Worship based in love is adornment. There is an interconnectedness between worship and gratitude. In the Bible, the Thessalonians worshipped idols believing they would get something: healthy crops, kids, health, long life, etc. They learned how to turn from these ineffective, under producing idols in exchange for worshipping and thanking the living God (I Thessalonians 1:9). Those who live Right Side Up lives leave a wake of gratitude to God (*Who do you thank?*) for their lives and circumstances (For *what* are you thankful?). Are you living a life of gratitude?

> *Sometimes I go to God and say, "God, if Thou dost never answer another prayer while I live on this earth, I will still worship Thee as long as I live and in the ages to come for what Thou hast done already." God's already put me so far in debt that if I were to live one million millenniums I couldn't pay Him for what He's done for me.*
> A.W. Tozer

Forgiveness

It may surprise you to discover this forgiveness portion in the "Spiritual," section and not the "Relationship," section. Frustration, hurt, betrayal and bitterness are everyday realities of living in a broken world. True forgiveness requires a supernatural understanding and power to release the perpetrators and unleash healing. If you were looking towards something or someone to fulfill a desire in you that they weren't designed to satisfy–you will hurt and hold that wound in your heart until you do something about it. Holding on to wounds and festering unforgiveness wreaks havoc on your life, keeping you from closeness and clear communication with those around you. Are you wanting to be free from the weight of bitterness and set your relationships up for success?

"He that cannot forgive others breaks the bridge over which he must pass himself; for every man has need to be forgiven."
Thomas Fuller

Q: Am I willing to let go of the PRIDE that is keeping my heart locked up?

Feelings of superiority hinder the process of forgiveness. The declaration, "I would have never done that!" can keep you in a prison of pride that will block true forgiveness. Understanding the frailty of humanity and having the courage to be humble are necessary companions on the road to forgiveness. Humility is also needed to stomp out hubris, enabling you the courage to seek forgiveness where you may have been hurtful or offensive to another. Are you willing to let go of your pride in order to experience the lightness of living in forgiveness?

> *"Forgiveness is the key which unlocks the door of resentment and the handcuffs of hatred. It breaks the chains of bitterness and the shackles of selfishness."*
> Corrie Ten Boom

Q: Do I understand the PATH of forgiveness?

Scaling a mountain is easier if there is a well worn path to follow. Forgiveness is similar, becoming more manageable when you can see the road that forgiveness moves down. It will help if you are mindful of the fact that forgiveness is a one-way street, something you can and need to do by yourself. Conversely, reconciliation is a two-way street, requiring the other party to do their part. Thankfully, Lewis Smedes shares 5 steps of forgiveness so that you can more easily identify where you are in the forgiveness process, helping you to see how much trail remains on the ascent towards a better relationship.

1. We hold the party responsible for their part.
2. We surrender our right to get even.
3. We revise our caricature of the person who harmed us.

4. We revise our feelings.
5. We accept the person who made us feel unacceptable.

Who do you need to forgive and what is your next step in your journey towards forgiveness?

"Forgiveness is not an emotion...Forgiveness is an act of will, and the will can function regardless of the temperature of the heart."
Corrie Ten Boom

Q: Do I understand the PRICE of forgiveness?

Forgiveness comes at a cost. When an injury is done, a debt is incurred that needs to be paid off. If the debt is paid–health, life, restoration and redemption are possible. If the debt isn't paid–frustration, victimization and continued woundedness and relational disruption are the result. Thankfully, you have a God who loves you more than His own life–someone who was willing to pay the debts that *you* had acquired. Gratefully, you have a God who was willing to pay a high price for the forgiveness He offers you with outstretched arms! How much did it cost your God to forgive you?

"As a Christian I am called to treat my enemy as a brother and to meet hostility with love. My behavior is thus determined not by the way others treat me, but by the treatment I receive from Jesus."
Dietrich Bonheoffer

Big

The biggest questions in life typically cross our minds when we are walking through difficult circumstances: the loss of a relationship, physical or emotional illness, a death in the family, a mid-life crisis or reaching the end of one's time on this earth. These life happenings float big questions to the surface of the conscious mind. The discerning among us learn how to become aware of these questions and regularly seek to discover their true and right answers. Wisdom and patience are a necessary part of wrestling well with these questions. Doing so will bring about good and fruitful seasons—the life we have always wanted to live!

> *"The boldness of asking deep questions may require unforeseen flexibility if we are to accept the answers."*
> Brian Greene

Q: Why am I worthy?

It is possible to be completely undeserving and completely worthy of God's love? Deservedness has to do with your *behavior*—worth has to do with your *being*. If you look to your circumstances for proof of your worth in God's eyes or His love for you—you're doomed! Worth is determined by what God sees in you, not in what you see in yourself. It is only at the cross where you can discover incontrovertible proof of your great worth and God's even greater love for you!

"I don't need to see my name in the credits at the end of a movie—my name is written in the book of life!"
Al Shier (Hollywood producer)

Q: When will I be lovable?

Feeling unlovable is one of the more common and unsavory feelings encountered. When I try to complete this statement, "I will be lovable when _____," I discover a long list of my dreams and pursuits which will never lead me to the love I crave. Why would those things, if accomplished, make me more lovable? When I put a time frame on love—I lose. As soon as I ask the, "when," question, I begin to point to an objective that needs to be achieved before I'm lovable. On the contrary, if I ask God this same question, He will simply smile, with the love of a Father who sees His child returning after a long journey away, and loudly pronounce, "I love you now! I always have and I always will!"

"My deepest awareness of myself is that I am deeply loved by Jesus Christ and I have done nothing to earn it or deserve it."
Brennan Manning

Q: When will I be enough?

An important follow-up question needs to be asked when exploring enoughness: *Good enough for what?* The question of sufficiency depends on the task at hand. Am I enough to swim to Catalina Island, perfectly love and lead my family or save myself on a cosmic level? No. That's my short answer. As I've thought, prayed and written in my journal for years, my conclusion on the matter is that though I may be capable of some things, it is *Jesus' enoughness* which makes me capable of being and doing all He has created me for and called me to be! Am I looking to be complete on my own or will the status and performance Jesus gives me enable me to know I am enough?

"If the world thinks you're not good enough, it's a lie, you know.
Get a second opinion."
Nick Vujicic

Sin

A h! Brave you are for embarking on this section. Good for you! Sin is infrequently discussed, yet often thought about. This little word carries much baggage. Often blamed by the secular world for mental disorder, relational disruptions and the general woes of the world, this lonely, neglected topic is vital to explore if health is what you desire. "Sin," is inherited, earned, sometimes enjoyable for a season, yet that which will trip you up most in life (Hebrews 12:1). If you are interested in improving your life, getting rid of the upside down life, take a look at what is ruling over you right now.

"You do not really care for God's mercy or His comfort
either, so long as you live in any sin. And it is well that you
do not; for you can have neither. Your peace will be like a
river, when you put away your sin; but not one word of true
peace, not one drop of true comfort, can you have till then."
Alexander Whyte

Q: When I think of the word, "Sin," what is the first thing that comes to mind?

If you thought of the sins of someone else, may I suggest you consider the sin of pride or judgment? When it comes to you and your life, what comes to mind? Did cheating on taxes, looking at or loving the wrong things come to mind? Maybe an area where you are missing the mark flashed across the marquee of your mind. Whatever popped into your head, whatever person, concept, circumstance or issue came to mind–God wants you to deal with it! Left unchecked, sin will destroy you and your relationships. What are you thinking and feeling nudged to deal with today?

"We drift toward compromise and call it tolerance; we drift toward disobedience and call it freedom; we drift toward superstition and call it faith. We cherish the indiscipline of lost self-control and call it relaxation; we slouch toward prayerlessness and delude ourselves into thinking we have escaped legalism; we slide toward godlessness and convince ourselves we have been liberated."
D.A. Carson

Q: What do I need to move towards?

In the same way that sin has a pervasive effect with hidden results, like ripples in a stream, the pursuit of God's best for you, *holiness*, also carries along with it a ripple of blessing and value that you may or may not see. Holiness, God and all that comes with Him, needs to increase in value. The longer term the goal, the healthier it is. Goals for today, for the next 5 years, for the next 20 years and into eternity can all be good if they move us towards God's best. What do you need to set your sights on if you want to live the best life possible?

"If your dreams develop in the process of seeking God's will and fit within His overall purposes, follow them. He would not have given them to you if they were not important."
Tony Dungy

Q: What's the difference between a morally restrained heart and a spiritually transformed heart? (Thanks Tim Keller for inspiring this question!)

I can live out of my own strength. I can parent out of my own energy, be a husband out of my own might and try to coach a sports team with my own vitality. And it won't be pretty. My energy will fade, bitterness will grow, my critical nature will pounce and my shame monster will win the day. Or, I can try to live life with the strength, power and perspective that the Holy Spirit brings me. I can try to avoid all the sin of the world with my own vigor, or, I can surrender to the only One who can help me live the life for which I ache. Who are we leaning on to live this life?

"Abide in Jesus, the sinless One – which means, give up all of self and its life, and dwell in God's will and rest in His strength. This is what brings the power that does not commit sin."
Andrew Murray

Q: What is it that I'm not believing about God or the gospel?

If you are sinning, you are failing to acknowledge who God really is, or what He has done for you. Through your life and relationship with the Father, you will discover His view on sin. Doesn't it seem like a good idea to have God's same heart and attitude towards the sin that can destroy you? In addition, you have probably experienced a season when you were incredibly in love. Other affections that were vying for your attention were wasting their time. So it is with the God and the message of the gospel. When you are so caught up in Him, as He is, your desire for lesser things fades away. What do you need to be reminded of today about who God is or what He has done for you?

"We are sinners simply because we choose to sin or live selfishly. We are never held accountable for what we are not the author of. Ability is always the measure of responsibility. God has given us the ability to direct our lives, either according to intelligence in recognition of our obligation to God and our fellowmen, or according to selfishness and unintelligence in the supreme seeking of our own happiness."
Gordon Olson

Pain & Suffering

We live in a broken world. The ease of the wonder years of childhood–being fed, taken care of, loved and protected, gives way to the reality of living in a world that can feel dangerous and unsafe at times. Pain is unavoidable, challenges are inevitable and the tension in our soul over the constant struggle we have with people and circumstances can way heavy on us. If we pause to consider for a few moments what life would be like if it were pain free, we would discover that it would also be void of other, beautiful things such as relationships and joy. God has blessed me with timely and reflective questions which have allow me to see His hand in trying times: What do I have now that I wouldn't have otherwise had if I hadn't suffered through this journey? Learning how to ask great questions will enable you to see ashes turned into beauty, fostering greater glory and honor for God!

"In light of heaven, the worst suffering on earth, a life full of the most atrocious tortures on earth, will be seen to be no more serious than one night in an inconvenient hotel."
Mother Theresa

Q: Am I willing to sit with and lean into painful moments?

Visiting us all, pain is no respecter of persons. No one is immune to the damaging effects of hurt and injury in our body, emotions, or relationships. In what universe does it make sense to, figuratively speaking, allow one's finger to continue to be burned by the fire of an open flame? Isn't it wise to pull it out and avoid the pain? Physically yes, but not always emotionally and relationally. Of course, some pain is so deep, it needs professional handling. But for many of us, learning how to sit with the discomfort of unwanted feelings or disconcerting relationships will allow us to discover a treasure map, leading us to a brighter and healthier life!

"The quickest way for anyone to reach the sun and the light of day is not to run west, chasing after the setting sun, but to head east, plunging into the darkness until one comes to the sunrise."
Gerald Sittser

Q: Am I willing to see obstacles as opportunities?

What if God loves you so much that He is willing to bring challenging circumstances, despicable people, or a testing child into your life? The apostle Paul spoke of rejoicing in sufferings (Romans 5:3-5), a foreign concept to those who work so hard to avoid pain and suffering. Like many wise people do, Paul seemed to embrace these trials and tribulations as opportunities. If this one word, "OPPORTUNITY," enters your mind during a painful moment or season, space will be created for God to bless you with His wisdom and His presence.

"Each day holds a surprise. But only if we expect it can we see, hear, or feel it when it comes to us. Let's not be afraid to receive each day's surprise, whether it comes to us as sorrow or as joy, it will open a new place in our hearts, a place where we can welcome new friends and celebrate more fully our shared humanity."
Henri Nouwen

Q: What if there is a purpose behind the pain?

Asked at the wrong time, this question will thrust greater pain and sorrow upon one's soul. But, when the time is right, and the scab has formed and dropped off, one can begin to look for the meaning, messages and lessons behind the scars. It is the height of arrogance to believe that just because I can't see a purpose for the pain, that there is no purpose for the pain. This question has allowed me to journey with pain towards a broader perspective and a deeper sense of meaning, giving way to a brighter and healthier life. How would our journey through life be different if we realized that a loving architect was leading and guiding us?

"Life is not a straight line leading from one blessing to the next and then finally to heaven. Life is a winding and troubled road. Switchback after switchback. And the point of biblical stories like

Joseph and Job and Esther and Ruth is to help us feel in our bones (not just know in our heads) that God is for us in all these strange turns. God is not just showing up after the trouble and cleaning it up. He is plotting the course and managing the troubles with far-reaching purposes for our good and for the glory of Jesus Christ."

John Piper

Where do we go from here?

My hope for this book is that you would read and re-read this book. Consider asking yourself three questions each day from a section. This book can function as either a resource guide in trying times or serve as a constant companion, questioning and prodding you towards life, health and God! These questions can point you in the right direction, give you the right motivation, but you are going to have to come up with strength from somewhere to make the choices and changes necessary for a Right Side Up life. Only you can do it—no one can do this for you.

"Courage is not simply one of the virtues,
the form of every virtue at the testing point."
CS Lewis

I challenge you to be courageous, lean into challenges, believe that God can move the mountains in your heart and life, ask great questions and be the best you can be! And so the question arises yet again—*Is a better life possible?*

Connection Point

Thank you for reading *Right Side Up!* I hope and pray that you will be challenged, inspired and use this book as a tool for growth for years to come!

I'd love to hear from you. Please let me know how I can serve you, your business, church or group. I am available for speaking engagements, seminars, retreats, as well as individual, couple and group coaching on a number of topics.

If you are interested, here is where you can find me:

http://www.flourishministries.org
craig@flourishministries.org

Flourish Ministries
P.O. Box 4012
Mission Viejo, CA 92690

I've been blessed to be a blessing. Let me know how I can serve you!

Craig L. Morris